Voc

By: Fr. William Doyle S.J.

"Pray ye therefore the Lord of the harvest,
that He send forth labourers into His harvest." - Matthew 9:38

Nihil Obstat: Joannes Keane, S.J.
        Cens. Theol. Dep.

Imprimi Potest: Eduardus
        Archiep. Dublinen., Dublini.
        Jan., 1928, Hiberniae Primas.

About The Author From The Publishers

We are about to give excerpts from a biography written by Alfred O'Rahilly on Fr. William Doyle S.J. This is what was reported in the newspaper about what happened to Fr. Doyle. "All through the worst hours an Irish padre went about among the dead and dying giving absolution to his boys. Once he came back to head quarters, but he would not take a bite of food or stay, though his friends urged him. He went back to the field to minister to those who were glad to see him bending over them in their last agony. Four men were killed by shell fire as he knelt beside them, and he was not touched not touched until his own turn came. A shell burst close by, and the padre fell dead."

Fr. Doyle had found the wounded officer lying far out in a shell crater. He crawled out to him, absolved and anointed him, and then, half dragging, half carrying the dying man, managed to get him within the line. Three officers came up at this moment, and McInespie was sent for some water. This he got and was handing it to Fr. Doyle when a shell burst in the midst of the group, killing Fr. Doyle and the three officers instantaneously, and hurling McInespie violently to the ground. Later in the day some of the Dublins when retiring came across the bodies of all four. Recognizing Fr. Doyle, they placed hint and a Private Meehan, whom they were carrying back dead, behind a portion of the Frezenberg.

Fr. Doyle met his death assigned to his Irish flock in spite of what they had suffered during the previous day. On 16th August 1917 the 16th Division made an advance along the Frezenberg ridge behind Ypres, where English Divisions had already failed several times.

The Publishers
8 September 2009
† Feast of the Birthday of the Blessed Virgin Mary

3

About The Author From The Publishers..3
I. Come, Follow Me...5
II. What is a Vocation?..6
III. Signs of a Vocation...9
IV. Motives for Entering Religion...10
V. Should We Encourage Vocations?...12
VI. Trying a Vocation...14
VII. Deliberation...17
VIII. Age for Entering..18
IX. Importance of Following a Vocation..20
X. Opposition...22
XI. Objections..24
XII. Advantages of Religious Life...29
XIII. The Harvest Of Souls..34
XIV. An Appeal..36
Appendix: Definitions 37

I. Come, Follow Me.

"Good Master, what good shall I do that I may have life everlasting?" It was the eager question of one whom fortune had blessed with the wealth of this world, but who realized that life eternal was a far more precious treasure. He had come to the Divine Teacher, seeking what he must yet do to make secure the great prize for which he was striving. He was young and wealthy, a ruler in the land, one whose life had been without stain or blemish.

"The Commandments? All these I have kept from my youth," he had said, "Good Master, what is yet wanting to me?"

Jesus looked on him with love, for such a soul was dear to His Sacred Heart. "If thou wilt be perfect," comes the answer, "go sell what thou hast and give to the poor, and come, follow Me."

There was a painful pause: nature and grace were struggling for the mastery; the invitation had been given, the road to perfection pointed out. There was only one sacrifice needed to make him a true disciple, but it was a big one, too great for him who lately seemed so generous. He hesitates, wavers, and then sadly turns away, with the words "Come, follow Me," ringing in his ears, for love of his "great possessions" had wrapped itself round his heart - a vocation had been offered and refused. "What a cloud of misgivings," says Father Faber, "must hang over the memory of him whom Jesus invited to follow Him. Is he looking now in Heaven upon that Face from whose mild beauty he so sadly turned away on earth?"

Nearly two thousand years have passed since then, but unceasingly that same Voice has been whispering in the ears of many a lad and maiden, "One thing is yet wanting to you - come, follow Me." Some have heard that voice with joy and gladness of heart, and have risen up at the Master's call; others have stop their ears, or turned away in fear from the side of Him Who beckoned to them, while not a few have stood and listened, wondering what it meant, asking themselves could such an invitation be for them, till Jesus of Nazareth passed by and they were left behind for ever.

To these, chiefly, is this simple explanation of a vocation offered, in the hope that they may recognize the workings of grace within their souls, or be moved to beg that they may one day be sharers in this crowning gift of God's eternal love.

II. What is a Vocation?

"How do I know whether I have a vocation or not?" How often this question has risen to the lips of many a young boy or girl, who has come to realize that life has a purpose, only to be brushed aside with an uneasy "I am sure I have not," or a secret prayer that they might be saved from such a fate! How little they know the happiness they are throwing away in turning from God's invitation, for such a question, and such a feeling, is often the sign of a genuine vocation.

In the first place, a vocation, or "a call to the priesthood or the religious life," in contradistinction to the general invitation, held out to all men, to a life of perfection even in the world, is a free gift of God bestowed on those whom He selects: "You have not chosen Me," He said to His Disciples, "but I have chosen you," and the Evangelist tells us that "Christ called unto Him whom He willed." Often that invitation is extended to those whom we would least expect. Magdalene, steeped to the lips in iniquity, became the spouse of the Immaculate; Matthew, surrounded by his ill gotten gains; Saul, "breathing out threatenings and slaughter against the Christians," each heard that summons, for a sinful life in the past, St. Thomas teaches, is no impediment to a vocation.

But though this gift is of surpassing value and a mark of very special affection on His part, God will not force its acceptance on the soul, leaving it free to correspond with the grace or reject it. Some day the Divine Hunter draws near the prey which He has marked out for the shafts of His love; timidly, as if fearing to force the free will, He whispers a word. If the soul turns away, Jesus often withdraws forever, for He only wants willing volunteers in His service. But if the startled soul listens, even though dreading lest that Voice speak again, and shrinking from what It seems to lead her to, grace is free to do its work and bring her captive to the Hunter's feet.

Unconsciously, in that first encounter, she has been deeply wounded with a longing for some unknown, as yet untasted, happiness. Almost imperceptibly a craving for a nobler life has taken possession of the heart; prayer and self denial, the thought of sacrifice, bring a new sweetness; the blazing light of earthly pleasures, once so dazzling, seems to die away; the joys, the amusements, of the world no longer attract or satisfy; their emptiness serves only to weary and disgust the more, while through it all the thirst for that indefinable "something" tortures the soul.

"Sweet and tender Lord!" exclaims the Blessed Henry Suso, "from the days of my childhood my mind has sought for something with burning thirst, but what it is I have not as yet fully understood. Lord, I have pursued it many a year, but I never could grasp it, for I know not what it is, and yet it is something that attracts my heart and soul, without which I can never attain true rest. Lord, I sought it in the first days of my childhood in creatures, but the more I sought it in them the less I found it, for every image that presented itself to my sight, before I wholly tried it, or gave myself quietly to it, warned me away thus: 'I am not what thou seekest.' Now my heart rages after it, for my heart would so gladly possess it. Alas! I have so constantly to experience what it is not! But what it is, Lord, I am not as yet clear. Tell me, Beloved Lord, what it is indeed, and what is its nature, that so secretly agitates me."

Even in the midst of worldly pleasure and excitement there is an aching void aching void in the heart. "How useless it all is! How hollow! How unsatisfying! Is this what my life is to be always? Was I made only for this?"

Slowly one comes to understand the excellence and advantage of evangelical perfection, the indescribable charm of virginity, and the nobleness of a life devoted wholly to the service of God and the salvation of souls. Louder and stronger has grown the faint whisper, "Come, follow Me," till at last, with an intense feeling of joy and gratitude, or even at times, a natural repugnance and fear of its responsibilities, the weary soul realizes that "The Master is here and calls for thee" that she has got a vocation.

A. True Vocation

A vocation, therefore, speaking generally, is not the mysterious thing some people imagine it to be, but simply the choice God makes of one for a certain kind of life.

"A person is known to have a true vocation to enter a particular career in life," writes Father C. Coppens, S.J., "if he feels sincerely convinced, as far as he can judge with God's grace, that such a career is the best for him to attain the end for which God places him on earth, and is found fit by his talents, habits and circumstances, to enter on that career with a fair prospect of succeeding in the same."

Père Poulain, S.J., the great French ascetical writer, adds: "In order to judge whether we have a vocation that is inspired by God, it is not usually sufficient to satisfy ourselves that we have a persistent attraction for it.

This mark is not certain unless a natural condition is fulfilled, namely, that we have certain physical, moral and intellectual qualities also."

A vocation to the religious state supposes, then, not only a supernatural inclination or desire to embrace it, but an aptitude or fitness for its duties. God cannot act inconsistently.

If He really wishes one to follow Him, He must give him the means of doing so, and hence if real obstacles stand in the way, e.g., serious infirmities, an old parent to support, etc., such a one is not called to enter religion.

God at times inspires a person to do something which He does not really wish or intend to be carried out. Thus David longed to build the Temple of the Lord; Abraham was told to sacrifice his son, merely to test their obedience and willingness; for, says St. Teresa, "God is sometimes more pleased with the desire to do a thing than with its actual accomplishment."

St. Francis de Sales regards "a firm and decided will to serve God" as the best and most certain sign of a true vocation, for the Divine Teacher had once said, "If you wish... come, follow Me." He writes: "A genuine vocation is simply a firm and constant will desirous of serving God, in the manner and in the place to which He calls me... I do not say this wish should be exempt from all repugnance, difficulty or distaste. Hence a vocation must not be considered false because he who feels himself called to the religious state no longer experiences the same sensible feeling which he had at first and that he even feels a repugnance and such a coldness that he thinks all is lost. It is enough that his will persevere in the resolution of not abandoning its first design.

In order to know whether God wills one to be a religious, there is no need to wait till He Himself speaks to us, or until He sends an angel from Heaven to signify His will; nor is there any need to have revelations on the subject, but the first movement of the inspiration must be responded to, and then one need not be troubled if disgust or coldness supervene."

III. Signs of a Vocation

The following is a list of some of the ordinary indications of a vocation, taken principally from the works of Father Gautrelet, S.J., and the Retreat Manual. No one need expect to have all these marks, but if some of them at least are not perceived, the person may safely say he has no vocation:

1. A desire to have a religious vocation, together with the conviction that God is calling you. This desire is generally most strongly felt when the soul is calm, after Holy Communion, and in time of retreat.

2. A growing attraction for prayer and holy things in general, together with a longing for a hidden life and a desire to be more closely united to God.

3. To have a hatred of the world, a conviction of its hollowness and insufficiency to satisfy the soul. This feeling is generally strongest in the midst of worldly amusement.

4. A fear of sin, into which it is easy to fall, and a longing to escape from the dangers and temptations of the world.

5. It is sometimes the sign of a vocation when a person fears that God may call them; when he prays not to have it and cannot banish the thought from his mind. If the vocation is sound, it will soon give place to an attraction, through Father Lehmkulhl says: "One need not have a natural inclination for the religious life; on the contrary, a divine vocation is compatible with a natural repugnance for the state."

6. To have zeal for souls. To realize something of the value of an immortal soul, and to desire to cooperate in their salvation.

7. To desire to devote our whole life to obtain the conversion of one dear to us.

8. To desire to atone for our own sins or those of others, and to fly from the temptations which we feel too weak to resist.

9. An attraction for the state of virginity.

10. The happiness which the thought of religious life brings, its spiritual helps, its peace, merit and reward.

11. A longing to sacrifice oneself and abandon all for the love of Jesus Christ, and to suffer for His sake.

12. A willingness in one not having any dowry, or much education, to be received in any capacity, is a proof of a real vocation.

IV. Motives for Entering Religion

St. Francis de Sales writes as follows: "Many enter religion without knowing why they do so. They come into a convent parlor, they see nuns with calm faces, full of cheerfulness, modesty and content, and they say to themselves: 'What a happy place this is! Let us come to it. The world frowns on us; we do not get what we want there.'

"Others come in order to find peace, consolation and all sorts of sweetness, saying in their minds: 'How happy religious are! They have got safe away from all their home worries; from their parents' continual ordering about and fault finding -- let us enter religion.'

"These reasons are worth nothing. Let us consider whether we have sufficient courage and resolution to crucify and annihilate ourselves, or rather to permit God to do so. You must understand what it is to be a religious. It is to be bound to God by the continual mortification of ourselves, and to live only for Him. Our heart is surrendered always and wholly to His Divine Majesty; our eyes, tongue, hands and all our members serve Him continually. Look well into your heart and see if you have resolution enough to die to yourself and to live only to God. Religion is nothing else than a school of renunciation and self mortification."

As the call to religious life is supernatural, a vocation springing solely from a purely human motive - such as those spoken of by St. Francis - the desire of pleasing one's parents, or some temporal advantage, would not be to work of grace. However, if the principal motive which inclines us to embrace the religious state is supernatural, the vocation is a true one, for Divine Providence often makes use of the trials and misfortunes of life to fill a soul with disgust for the world and prepare it for a greater grace.

St. Romuald, founder of the Camaldolese, to escape the consequences of a duel in which he had taken part, sought an asylum in a monastery, where he was so struck by the happy lives of the monks that he consecrated himself to God.

St. Paul, the first hermit, fled to the desert to avoid persecution, and found in the solitude a peace and joy he had sought in vain. How many eyes have been rudely opened to the shortness and uncertainly of life by the sudden death of a dear friend, and made to realize that the gaining of life eternal was "the one thing necessary"; thwarted ambition, the failure of cherished hopes or the disappointment of a loving heart, have convinced many a future saint that the only Master worth serving is Jesus Christ, His affection the only love worth striving for.

Hence we may conclude with the learned theologian, Lessius, "If anyone takes the determination of entering religion, well resolved to observe its laws and duties, there is no doubt that his resolution, this vocation, comes from God, whatever the circumstances which seem to have produced it."

"It matters little how we commence, provided we are determined to persevere and end well," says St. Francis de Sales; and St. Thomas lays it down that "no matter from what source our resolution comes of entering religion, it is from God"; while Suarez maintains that "generally the desire for religious life is from the Holy Ghost, and we ought to receive it as such."

V. Should We Encourage Vocations?

It is a curious fact that although many pious and learned persons do not shrink from discouraging, in every possible way, aspirants to religious life, they would scruple to give them any help or encouragement. "A vocation must be entirely the work of the Holy Ghost," they say. Willingly they paint the imaginary difficulties and trials of a convent life, and hint at the unhappiness sometimes to be found there; they speak of the long and serious deliberation necessary before one takes such a step, and thus, unintentionally perhaps, but most effectively extinguish the glowing enthusiasm of a youthful heart.

Some even assume a terrible responsibility by deliberately turning away souls from the way into which the master is calling them, forgetting the warning: "It is I who have chosen you," never reflecting on the irretrievable harm they are causing by spoiling the work of God.

Others calmly assure a postulant, who has been found unsuitable for a particular Order, that this is a certain sign Almighty God does not want him, that he has no vocation and should not try again.

It is quite true to say that a vocation comes from above, but God's designs can be hindered or helped by His creatures, and He has ever made use of secondary agents in their execution. The formation of character and the direction of the steps of the young towards the sanctuary is largely in the hands of parents and teachers; how many a happy priest and nun daily thank their Maker for the gift of a good mother, who first sowed the seeds of a vocation in their childish heart. Fathers and mothers constantly put before their children the various calling and professions of life to help them in the choice; is the grandest life of all, the service of the King of Kings, the battling for precious souls, and the extension of Christ's Kingdom, to be ignored and never spoken of?

The Saints realized that God looked to them to aid Him in the work of fostering vocations. St. Jerome writes thus to Heliodorus: "I invite you, make haste. You have made light of my entreaties; perhaps you will listen to my reproaches. Effeminate soldier! What are you doing under the paternal roof? Hasten to enlist under the banner of Christ."

So eloquently did St. Bernard speak of the advantages of the religious life that all his brothers and thirty young nobles followed him to the solitude of Citeaux.

More striking still was the bringing of the Apostles to Our Lord by indirect means. St. Andrew and St. John were sent to the Saviour by St.

John the Baptist: "Behold the Lamb of God. And the two disciples heard him speak, and they followed Jesus."

"Andrew findeth first his brother Simon, and he brought him to Jesus."

"On the following day he (Andrew) would go forth into Galilee, and he findeth Philip... Philip findeth Nathaniel, and said to him: We have found Him of Whom the prophets did write... and Nathaniel said to him: Can any good come out of Nazareth? Philip said to him: Come and see," with the result that he also received the call to follow Christ.

Thus one by one the Apostles were brought to the knowledge of the Messias and under the influence of His grace, without which all human efforts are useless to produce a vocation. "Know well," says St. Thomas, "that whether it be the suggestion of the devil or the advice of a man which inclined us to the religious life, and makes us thus walk in the footsteps of Jesus Christ, this suggestion or advice is powerless and inefficient so long as God does not attract us inwardly towards Him. Therefore, the proposal of entering into religion, in whatever way it may be suggested to us, can come only from God."

"No man can come to Me, unless it can be given him by My Father." Hence the Saint adds, that even if the religious vocation came from devil, it ought to be embraced as an excellent counsel given by an enemy.

VI. Trying a Vocation

Spiritual writers tell us the evil spirit strives in every possible way to hinder all the good he can. If he cannot turn one away completely from the determination of giving oneself to God, he will work, might and main, to defer the moment as long as possible, knowing that a person in the world is constantly exposed to the danger of losing both the grace of God and "the pearl of great price," his vocation. He knows that until the doors of the monastery have closed behind the young Levite he has every chance of snatching away that treasure. He will lay traps and pitfalls, stir up doubts and fears; he will make the attractions of a life of pleasure seem almost irresistible, causing the bravest heart to waver: "I never realized how dear the world to me until I had to leave it" has been the agonizing cry of many.

Under one pretext or another he induces them to put off their generous resolution from day to day. "O Lord," exclaims St. Augustine, "I said I will come presently; wait a moment; but this presently never came, and this moment did not end. I always resolved to give myself to You on the morrow, and never immediately."

How fatal this delay in responding to the call of God has been those can best tell whom age or altered circumstances have hindered from carrying out their first intention.

If the vocation is doubtful, there is need of deliberation, and it must be serious, for hastiness and want of reflection would be unpardonable in such a matter; but so enormous are the advantages to be reaped from a life devoted to God's service, it would be a far greater calamity to miss a vocation through excessive prudence than to mistake a passing thought for the Master's call.

It is well to remember that a person who felt he had no vocation would not sin by embracing the religious state, provided he had the intention of fulfilling all its obligations and serving God to the best of his ability. For, in the opinion of the Angelic Doctor, God will not refuse the special graces, necessary for such a life, to one who sincerely desires to promote His glory.

Our Lord tells us to learn a lesson from "the children of this world, who are wiser in their generation"; there is no hesitation about accepting a tempting offer of marriage, which binds one, perhaps to an unsuitable partner, for life; it is worldly wisdom not to delay about such a step when there is a chance of being well settled; and yet St. Ignatius teaches that there is more need for deliberation about remaining in the world than for leaving it. He says: "If a person thinks of embracing a secular life, he should ask and desire more evident signs that God calls him to a secular life than if there were question of embracing the Evangelical Counsels. Our Lord Himself has exhorted us to embrace His Counsels, and, on the other hand, He has laid before us the great dangers of a secular life ; so that, if we rightly conclude, revelations and extraordinary tokens of His will are more necessary for a man entering upon a life in the world than for one entering the religious state."

Endless harm has been done by well meaning people, who, under pretext of "trying a vocation", keep their children from entering a religious house for years.

They urge that getting "to know the world" will develop their faculties and enable them to understand their own mind better; that such a process will broaden their views and help them to judge things at their proper value; finally, that a vocation which cannot stand such a trial, the buffeting of dangerous temptations, and the seductive allurements of worldly pleasure, to which it has been unnecessarily exposed, is no vocation and had far better be abandoned.

"Is the world the place for testing a vocation?" asks St. Vincent de Paul. "Let the soul hasten as fast as possible to secure asylum." The Church, realizing well the necessity of such a trial, prescribes at least a year of probation in every novitiate before admitting candidates to the religious profession. There, safe from the contagious atmosphere of a corrupt world, with abundant time for prayer and thought, with liberty to remain or leave at will, each one can test for himself the sincerity of the desire he felt to abandon all things and follow Christ, before he binds himself irrevocably by his vows.

"One could not give a more pernicious counsel than this," writes Father Lessius. "What is it in reality except the desire to extinguish the interior spirit, under the pretext of a trial, and to expose to the tempest of temptation him who was preparing to gain the port of safety?

"If a gardener were to plant a precious seed, requiring great care, in stony ground, covered with thorns; if he exposed it to the rays of the sun and every change of climate to try would it grow in that unfavorable spot, who would not look upon him as a fool? Those who advise people called to religious life to remain, for a while, in the world have even less sense. A vocation is a divine fruit for eternal life. It is planted in the human heart, a soil little suited to its nature, and requires great care and attention. Watch must be kept that the birds of the air, the demons, do not carry it away; that thorns, the concupiscences and solicitudes of the world, do not choke it; that men with their false maxims should not trample it under foot. Whosoever wishes to preserve and see grow in his heart the seed which the Divine Sower has cast there, ought to fly from the world and reach a safe refuge as soon as possible."

VII. Deliberation

It follows from what has been said that once the voice of God is recognized, that is when the thought of leaving the world has been more or less constantly before the mind for some time, and the souls realizes, even though she dreads it, that "the Lord hath need of her," the call ought to be obeyed promptly.

St. Thomas holds that the invitation to a more perfect life ought to be followed without delay, for these lights and inspirations from God are transient, not permanent, and therefore the divine call should be obeyed instantly. As of old, when He worked His miracles and went about doing good, "Jesus of Nazareth passeth by"; if we do not take advantage of His passing, He may never return. "I stand at the door and knock," He said, "If any man shall hear My voice and open to Me, I will come in to him," if not, that call may never come again.

"Make haste, I beseech you," exclaims St. Jerome, "and rather cut than loosen the rope by which your bark is bound fast to the land," for even a day's delay deprives a person of invaluable merit, which he would acquire in religion.

Delay is dangerous, and long deliberation, as Msgr. Malou assures us, is unnecessary: "Of all the state of life the religious state is, without contradiction, that which demands the least deliberation, and is that of which the choice should cause less doubt, and provoke the least hesitation; for it is in this state that fewer difficulties are met with, and the best means are found for saving our souls."

VIII. Age for Entering

"It is well for a man to have borne the yoke from his youth," says Holy Scripture. Mindful of this counsel, and realizing that the pure heart of the young receive the impressions of virtue without difficulty, and easily form good habits, that it is above all the time of earnestness and generosity, the Church has always encouraged her children to give themselves to her service from their tender years. The Council of Toledo laid it down: "As soon as a child has arrived at adolescence, that is to say, at the age of twelve for girls and fourteen for boys, they may freely dispose of themselves by entering religion." It is not forbidden to enter at any age; the Council of Trent simply ordained that no one should be admitted to profession before the age of sixteen years completed, but it did not forbid entrance before that time.

Special provision was made in the Rule of St. Benedict for the admission of little children, who were offered by their parents to be educated and thereafter perpetually to persevere in the Order.

"The reception of a child in those days was almost as solemn as a profession in our own. His parents carried him to the church. Whilst they wrapped his hand, which held the petition, in the sacred linen of the altar, they promised, in the presence of God and of His Saints, stability in his behalf. Little beings of three or four years old were brought in the arms of those who gave them life, to accept at their bidding the course in which that life was to run. They were brought into the sanctuary, received the cowl, and took their places as monks in the monastic community."

St. Benedict was only twelve when he entered the cloister, and St. Thomas of Aquinas barely fourteen. St. Catherine of Ricci was professed at thirteen; Blessed Imelda died in a Dominican Convent at the age of eleven, and St. Rose of Lima had vowed her chastity to God while only five. In our own days Sœur Therese, "The Little Flower," was scarcely fifteen when she entered the Carmelite monastery at Lisieux.

"The Spirit breatheth where He will." There is no rule for vocations, no age limit for the call. Innocence attracts the gaze of God, deep rooted habits of sin, provided they are not persevered in, do not always repel Him. One comes because of the world disgusts him, another loves it and leaves it with regret; docility draws down more graces, while resistance often increases the force of His invitation. The little child hears His whisperings, while others have not been summoned till years were far advanced.

So jealous is the Church of this liberty for her children that the Council of Trent excommunicates those who, by force or fear, hinder anyone from entering religion without just cause.

As parents often exceed the authority given them by God over their children, in the question of a choice of life, it will be well here to quote the words of the great Jesuit Moralist, Father Ballerini: "Paternal power cannot take away the right which sons and daughters have to make their own choice of a state of life, and, if they will, to follow Christ's Counsels. The duty, however, which filial piety demands ought not to be disregarded, and the leave of parents ought to be asked. If it is refused, their children ought not at once to take their departure, but should wait for some little time till the parents have realized their obligations. If, however, there should be danger of the parents unjustly hindering the fulfillment of their children's vocation, they may and ought to go without their parent's knowledge. Parents have a right to make some trial of the vocation of their children before they enter; it is not, however, lawful for them to insist that they should first taste the pleasure of the world. If they should happen to be affected by these, the parent would not have reason to conclude that there had not been a true vocation. There may be a true vocation which has been wrongfully abandoned."

St. Liguori quotes a number of theologians who hold that "Parents who prevent their children from entering religion sin mortally." "To turn one from a religious vocation," says St. Jerome, "is nothing else than to slay Jesus Christ in the heart of another."

19

IX. Importance of Following a Vocation

There is no more important moment in the life of a young boy or girl than when "they stand with trembling feet" at the parting of the ways. With St. Paul they had said: "When I was a child, I spoke as a child, I thought as a child," but the days of irresponsible childhood are gone forever, and now they must launch their bark alone on the stormy waters of life and steer their course of eternity. It is a solemn moment, a time big with possibilities for good or evil, for the youth is face to face with question what he must do with his future life, a choice upon which not merely his happiness on earth, but even his eternal salvation, may depend.

He has been made by his Creator and given a precious gift to spend it in a certain, definite way, marked out from all eternity by the hand of Divine Providence. What that life is to be for many, circumstances and surroundings clearly indicate. But in the hearts of others arises a violent storm from the clashing of rival interests.

On the one hand comes the call of the world, the pleading of human nature for a life of ease and pleasure; on the other, the Voice of Christ, softly yet clearly, "Come, follow Me - I have need of you - I have work for you to do."

This, then, is the meaning of his life, the reason why he was drawn out of nothingness, "to work the works of Him Who sent Him." Is he free to hesitate? Is it a matter of indifference for him to live in a God chosen state of life or in a self chosen one, now that his vocation is certain?

To this question St. Liguori answers: "Not to follow our vocation, when we feel called to the religious state, is not a mortal sin; the Counsel of Christ, from their nature, do not oblige under this penalty. However, in regard to the dangers to which our salvation is exposed, in choosing a state of life against the Divine Will, such conduct is rarely free from sin, much more so when a person is persuaded that in the world he places himself in danger of losing his soul by refusing to follow his vocation."

Though one would not sin mortally by refusing to follow a clear vocation, since it is an invitation, not a command, a person would certainly run a great risk of imperiling his salvation by so acting. God foresees the temptations and dangers of each one; some He knows would never save their souls in the midst of a sinful world, and these He calls away to protect them from its dangers. To the vocation He has attached helps and graces to strengthen the weak soul, but deprived of this help -- for God may refuse to give them in the world the graces He would have granted in religion -- many will find salvation extremely difficult.

Hence, though the deliberate refusal to correspond to the Divine vocation does not necessarily imply the commission of sin, even when the call is clear and unmistakable, yet it is a serious responsibility, without sufficient reason, to refuse to correspond to such an invitation, offered with so much love and liberality; for a vocation not only shows God's eagerness for the sanctification of the person called to follow in His footsteps, but implies that the Savior looks for his constant cooperation in "the divinest of all works," the salvation of human souls.

Can it be wondered at, then, that, deprived of the special graces destined for them, the lives of those who have refused to follow, or have abandoned, a decided vocation are generally unhappy, and, too often, as every confessor knows, sullied with great and numerous sins?

X. Opposition

Seeing the immense importance of a vocation, and how much depends upon it, both for ourselves and others, it is only natural to expect that the evil one should stir up a regular hornet's nest of opposition. He will prevent it if he can and will not give up the fight without a fierce struggle. Checked and defeated in one direction, he renews his attacks, with greater audacity, in another, striving by delays, disappointments and interior trials to weary the soul and turn it in the end from its resolve. It has been truly said that we never fully realize the number of enemies we have to contend with until the moment we make up our mind resolutely to serve God. One certainly never knew how many people were so keenly interested in our future happiness, so anxious to warn us of the difficulties and dangers of our proposed step, until it became known we were entering religion.

When a young man resolves to renounce the world, his so called friends rally round him begging of him not to be such a coward as to run away from what clearly is his duty. They remind him of all the good he might do by staying where he is, but his conscience assures him there is nothing better he can do than go where God, his Master, bids him. They ask him if he is he a mad fool to give up all the amusements and pleasures he might lawfully enjoy; would it not be better for him first "to see life," before he buries himself in a gloomy cloister; they taunt him with want of moral courage and call him hard hearted and cruel to desert a loving father or mother in their declining years.

What a terrific struggle it all is he only knows who has been through it. To be told one is simply selfish when one wants only to be generous; to meet with nothing but coldness, cynicism and discouragement when most of all there is an agonizing cry in the soul for kindness and sympathy, is hard indeed for flesh and blood to bear, even for the love of Jesus. God, too, Who at first "had disposed all things sweetly" to wean the soul from earthly love and draw it to Himself, in the end sometimes seems to hide His face and abandon His spouse. "It seemed to me," the holy Mother Kerr used to say, "that all my wish for religious life vanished from the moment I decided to follow it."

Doubts and fears give place to the joy and yearning for a life of sacrifice, which formerly filled the heart. St. Teresa, however, tells us not to fear, for this trial, if bravely borne, will lead to greater happiness.

"When an act is done for God alone," she writes, "it is His will before we begin it that the soul, in order to increase its merit, should be afraid; and the greater the fear, if we do but succeed, the greater the reward and the sweetness thence afterwards resulting. I know this from experience; and so, if I had to advise anybody, I would never counsel anyone, to whom good inspirations may come, to resist them through fear of the difficulty of carrying them into effect; there is no reason of being afraid of failure since God is omnipotent.

"Though I could not at first bend my will to be a nun, I saw that the religious state was the best and safest. And thus, by little and little, I resolved to force myself into it. The struggle lasted three months. I used to press this reason against myself: The trials and sufferings of living as a nun cannot be greater than those of Purgatory, and I have well deserved to be in Hell. It is not much to spend the rest of my life as if I were in Purgatory, and then go straight to Heaven. The devil put before me that I could not endure the trials of religious life, because of my delicate nature. I was subject to fainting fits, attended with fever, for my health was always weak. I defended myself against him by alleging the trials which Christ endured, and that it was not too much for me to suffer something for His sake; besides, He would help me to bear it. I remember perfectly well that the pain I felt when I left my father's house was so great (he would never give his consent to my entering) that I do not believe the pain of dying will be greater, for it seemed to me as if every bone in my body were wrenched asunder. When I took the habit, Our Lord at once made me understand how He helps those who do violence to themselves, in order to serve Him, I was filled with a joy so great that it has never failed me to this day."

XI. Objections

To make matters worse, we play into the hands of the tempter by listening to his objections, or building up for ourselves imaginary difficulties, which may never occur, forgetting that with the call comes the special "grace of vocation," with which, as the Apostles assures us, "we can do all things."

1. "I may not persevere." Were one to hesitate before a possible failure, little would be done in the world, but the Church wisely guards against this danger by giving the aspirant to Religion ample time, in the noviceship, to try if he is really called or suited for such a life. To leave or be dismissed from the house of probation is no disgrace, but simply shows God has other designs on the soul. St Joseph of Cupertino was several times refused admission into the Franciscan Order as unsuitable, He entered the Capuchins, but was sent away, after eight months trial, because it was thought he had no vocation. Out of compassion he was then received by the Franciscans, with whom he lived till his saintly death.

Suarez tells us we are to consider less our own strength in the matter than the help of grace, for it is in God we must particularly trust. He will not desert us if only we are faithful to His inspirations. If He calls those who do not seek Him, much more will He aid and protect those who have obeyed His call.

"If I did but know that I should persevere," says the author of the Imitation, "and presently he heard within himself an answer from God: 'Do now what thou wouldst do then, and thou shalt be very secure.'"

"Instead of being frightened at the sight of a few who have been inconstant in their vocation," St. John Chrysostom says, "why not consider the great number of those who, faithful to their engagements, find in religion peace, happiness and salvation?"

2. "My health may break down." No religious is ever dismissed, after profession, through ill health. Should God not give sufficient strength for the duties of the novitiate, it is an evident sign that He wants the novice elsewhere. Thus St. Benedict Joseph Labre, finding himself unable to persevere with either the Cistercians or Carthusians, and having tried in vain, for two years, to enter among the Trappists, saw that his vocation lay in another direction, the perfect imitation, in the world, of the humble, suffering life of the Master. Experience has proved in numberless cases that the regular Community life is of immense benefit to those of feeble health, and God rewards the generous spirit and trust of one willing to serve Him in the midst of infirmities, by giving new vigor and strength.

Pere Surin, S.J. advised his mother to become a Carmelite nun at the age of fifty six. So delicate had she been that she required the constant attendance of four nurses, yet during the fifteen years she lived in the convent, observing all the austerities of the Rule, she never once entered the infirmary.

Another Carmelite, Madame Soyecourt, who died at the age of eighty, had never even abstained in the world on account of ill health.

St. Bernard served God faithfully for sixty three years, never relaxing his penances, fasting or labors, though from his entry into religion he was extremely delicate and constantly spat blood.

3. "I should break my parent's heart." When the devil sees in anyone a religious vocation, he does everything possible to prevent him following that attraction. But of all the means he makes use of, the love of one's parents is the most powerful and dangerous. He shows it to be so just and reasonable, he makes use of such specious sophisms, that the poor soul does not know to which voice to listen - that which call him or that which bids him go back.

St. Alphonsus Liguori declared that the hardest trial of all his life was when he made known to his father his determination of quitting the world. "Dear father, I see that you suffer for my sake. However, I must declare that I no longer belong to this world: God has called me, and I am determined to follow His voice." For three hours the father clasped him in his arms weeping and repeating, "My son, do not leave me! Oh, my son, my son! I do not deserve this treatment." If he had listened to this pathetic appeal the Church would have lost one of her grandest saints; fortunately he remembered the words of Him Who could call Himself "the kindest and gentlest of men." "Do not think that I came to send peace upon earth: I came not to send peace but the sword. For I came to separate the son from the father, and the daughter from the mother; ... he that loveth father or mother more than Me is not worthy of Me."

A terrible responsibility rest on the conscience of some parents, who, through selfishness or misguided love, succeed in preventing their children from following the call of God, and unscrupulously withhold from Him those He is drawing to Himself.

They may have the satisfaction of keeping a little longer with them those to whom they have given birth, but they must answer one day to their Judge for the immense good they have hindered, and the souls of those lost through their fault.

Though it meant a big sacrifice, even a serious loss, no right minded father would dream for a moment of forbidding a marriage which would bring to his child joy and good fortune; why then interfere with that holy alliance, made in Heaven, which means far greater happiness?

St. Ambrose asks if it is just that a young girl should have less liberty in choosing God for her Spouse that she has in selecting an earthly one.

To the mother of a family who opposes the religious vocation of her daughter one might say: "You married, and you did well. Had you been forced to enter a convent, would you have done it?"

4. "I could do more good in the world." In a very exceptional case, and under circumstances not likely to be realized, this might be true, but such a statement generally shows a want of realization of the immense advantages of religious life, and the merit which comes from the living vows.

Would St. Francis, St. Dominic, or St. Ignatius have done more for God's glory had they led the life of pious laymen, and would not the world have been poorer and Heaven emptier if Nano Nagle, Catherine Macaule or Mary Aikenhead had refused the grace offered them?

5. "Good people are wanted in the world." But does God want me there? If so, why did He give me a call to leave it? Surely I must take it for granted that He knows what is best for me and for His glory, and blindly follow His voice.

Pere Olivaint, one of the Jesuit Martyrs of the Commune, answers the objection of a young man who wished to remain in the world as follows: "My parents have plans for my future... But what does God want? In that position which is offered to me men will hold me in great esteem... But God? My natural taste moves me in that direction... But God? I shall certainly be able to save my soul in the world... True, but does God wish that you should save it there?"

Granting that I have a clear vocation to the religious life, where I shall be far better able and more fitted to work for the welfare of my neighbor, I cannot persuade myself that I could do more good by going against the Will of God.

6. "I may be unhappy in the convent." Is the world, then, such an earthly paradise, so full of love, peace and happiness that no sorrows is to be found there? Religious may have much to suffer, days of trial and desolation to be endured, the grinding monotony of a never changing round of duties to be bravely faced, day by day, yet with St. Paul they can exclaim: "I superabound with joy in the midst of my tribulations."

"Father," said an old Trappist monk, "I have so much consolation here amid all our austerities I fear I shall have none in the next world."

"One evening in winter," writes the Little Flower, "I was about my lowly occupation; it was cold and dark. Suddenly I heard the harmony of several musical instruments outside the convent, and pictured to myself a richly furnished, brilliantly lit drawing-room, resplendent with gilding and decorations; young ladies, tastefully dressed were sitting there and paying each other many a vain compliment. Then I looked on the poor invalid I was tending. For the music I had her complaints; for the gilded drawing room, the brick walls of an austere convent, lighted only by a feeble glimmer. The contrast was exceedingly sweet. The dim light of earthly joys was denied me, but the light of God shone all around. No, I would not have bartered those ten minutes taken by my deed of charity for ten thousand years of worldly diversions."

"Here in Carmel," she adds, "a prey to bodily and spiritual anguish, I am happier than I was in the world; yes, happier even than in my home, and by my beloved father's side."

7. "Perhaps I never had a vocation." Many persons have been tried by great doubts about their vocation, sometimes fearing they had deceived themselves, and that it would be impossible for them to secure their salvation in the religious state. All sweetness and devotion seems to have vanished; everything is wearisome, prayer, spiritual reading, even recreation, a clear sign, they think, that God never wished them to enter!

Theologians, and at their head St. Liguori, lay it down as a principle that even if one should enter religion without a vocation and persevere through the novitiate, God will certainly give one at the moment of pronouncing one's vows. To hesitate or doubt when that step has been taken would be treason: "He who puts his hand to the plough and looks back, is not worthy of Me."

Moreover, that repugnance and even dislike, which some suffer from during the whole of their religious life, is not a sign of want of vocation, if they persevere; God is only trying their fidelity to increase their merit.

8. "Wait! Wait! Wait! If I were you I would not be in such a hurry." But Jesus would not let the young man remain even to bury his father: "Let the dead bury their dead," He said, "and come thou and follow Me make haste and tarry not."

"You do not know the world." I know it is my worst foe, the friend and helper of my deadly enemy, Satan, and a danger I should fear and fly from.

"You are too young, wait a while." Should I wait till the foul breath of the world has tarnished the beauty of the lily of my soul, which God loves for its spotless purity and wants for Himself. "It is well for a man who has borne the yoke from his youth."

XII. Advantages of Religious Life

Within the limits of a small pamphlet it would be impossible to give even an outline of the advantages of the religious state, and the heavenly favors enjoyed by those who are called to such a life. "What a glorious kingdom of the Holy Ghost is the religious state!" writes Father Meschler, S.J. "It is like an island of peace and calm in the middle of the fleeting, changing, restless flood of this earthly life. It is like a garden planted by God and blessed with the fat of the land and the dew of heavenly consolation. It is like a lofty mountains where the last echoes of this world are still, and the first sounds of the blessed eternity are heard. What peace, what happiness, purity and holiness has it shed over the face of the earth."

Nor is this to be wondered at, since God is never outdone in generosity, rewarding the sacrifices made in obedience to His call with a lavish hand.

Peter said to Him: "Behold, we have left all things, and have followed Thee: what, therefore, shall we have?" And Jesus said to them: "You shall receive a hundredfold and possess life everlasting."

"Taste and see how sweet the Lord is," says the Psalmist, for only those who have experience of the happiness, peace and contentment of the cloister realize fully the truth of the Savior's words: "Mary hath chosen the better part." The present writer could quote the heartfelt words of gratitude to God from many a soul for the grace of their vocation. One who had to suffer much in breaking the ties which bound her to the world and home, writes: "I seem to be slowly awakening from a long dream. I am so very happy I do not know if I am myself or some one else. How can I ever thank God enough for bringing me here?"

St. Jerome compares religious, who have left the world, to the Israelites delivered from the bondage of Egypt, and says God has shown great love for them in exchanging their hard slavery for the sweet liberty of the children of God.

A. Its Happiness

Many caricatures have been painted of monks and nuns, depicting them as a merry, jovial crew, rejoicing in the good things of this world, but no artist has ever yet drawn a religious community as a collection of sad faced, melancholy beings. The very atmosphere of a convent is joy and tranquility, its inmates bright and cheerful; for, safe from the storms and troubles of the world and the insatiable desire for wealth, free from the cares, the anxieties, of a home and family, protected by the mantle of a loving charity from the disputes, the quarrels and petty jealousies of life, they have at last found true happiness, which consists in peace of soul and contentment of heart.

The world may boast of many things, but it cannot claim to give happiness to its followers. One who had the means of gratifying every craving, Solomon, sadly exclaimed: "Whatsoever my heart desired, I refused them not, and I withheld not my heart from enjoying every pleasure, but I saw in all things only vanity and vexation of spirit, except to love God and serve Him alone."

The life of a religious, like that of every other human being, must be a warfare to the end; they have their crosses and tribulations, and God, in order to sanctify them, often sends great trials and interior sufferings, yet through it all, deep down in the soul they feel the presence of Christ's most precious gift: "My peace I leave you, My peace I give you," that peace of heart, "a continual feast," which the world knows not of, nor can earthly pleasures bestow.

Hence St. Lawrence Justinian says: "Almighty God has designedly concealed the happiness of religious life, because if it were known all will relinquish the world and fly to religion."

"An earthly Paradise," says St. Mary Magdalen of Pazzi and St. Scholastica, "If men knew the peace which religious enjoy in retirement, the entire world would become one great convent."

Secure in the possession of God, rejoicing in the promise of a glorious eternity, is it any wonder that those who left all to follow Christ should find "His yoke sweet and His burden light"? The writer of Recit d'une Sœur sums up well this picture of true religious life in these words: "Happiness in heaven purchased by happiness on earth."

B. Its Holiness

Spiritual writers say that life in religion surpasses all others, because it removes obstacles to perfection and consecrates one, in the most perfect manner, to God. The world, with its round of amusements and distractions is the deadly enemy of piety, and even the best disposed persons find it hard not to be influenced by the prevailing spirit of indifference to spiritual things, or unaffected by so much careless, if not downright evil, example around them. Many a holy soul hungers for prayer and recollection, only to find that the cares of a family, the calls of social duties, the unavoidable visits and entertainment, encroach far on the limited time they can give to God.

In religion, on the other hand, care of the soul is the first and most important duty, its advancement and perfection the great business of life.

By a wise economy of time, religious, in spite of many other occupations, can devote four or five hours a day to meditation, prayer, visits to the Blessed Sacrament, and the recitation of the Office, so well distributed that no burden is felt.

His rules and the voice of obedience make known to him the Will of God, which he could never be certain of in the world; they protect him from a multitude of dangerous temptation, shutting out in great measure the possibility of sin; the company of so many chosen souls, their generous example and saintly lives, spur him on to nobler things; saved from all worldly anxieties, he can give his whole heart to the service and love of God, leading a life which is an earnest, if humble, imitation of his Lord and Master Jesus Christ.

"O Lord," cries out holy David, "a single day in Thy house is worth a thousand in the courts of sinners." "I hold it for certain," says St. Alphonsus, "that the greatest number of the vacant thrones of the fallen Seraphim will be occupied by souls sanctified in the religious state. Among the sixty persons canonized during the last century there were only five who did not belong to religious orders."

C. The Triple Cord: The Vows

But that which constitute the essence of religious life, and give to it such merit, is the observance of the three vows of evangelical perfection - poverty, chastity and obedience. A vow is a solemn promise made to God, after serious deliberation and having fully grasped its responsibilities, by which the soul engages to perform something, under pain of sin, which is better to do than to omit.

It is certain that it is more perfect and more agreeable to God to do a good work, after having obliged ourselves to do it by vow, than to do it freely without this obligation. For, as St. Thomas says, an act of perfect virtue is always of itself more excellent than that of a lesser virtue. Thus, an act of charity is more meritorious than an act of mortification, since charity is a more perfect virtue than the virtue of penance. After the theological virtues of faith, hope and charity, the most perfect of all is the virtue of religion, by which we worship God; a vow is an act of this the noblest of all the moral virtues, the virtue of religion, and by it all the actions performed in virtue of the vows are elevated to the dignity of acts of religion, giving them not only much greater value in the eyes of God and imparting to the will constancy and firmness in well doing, but immensely increasing the holiness of the person, since from each action he reaps a double reward, the merit of the act of virtue, and the merit of the act of religion, imparted by the vow.

Of all the vows that can be made, the three of the religious state are the noblest and the best. The perfection of a Christian consists in renouncing the cupidities of life, in trampling on the world, in breaking all ties that hold him captive, and in being bound and united to God by perfect charity. The three great obstacles that prevent him from acquiring this perfection are, according to St. John, the concupiscence of the eyes for riches, the concupiscence of the flesh for the pleasure of the senses, and the pride of life for seeking after honors. The vow of poverty destroys the first, the vow of chastity the second, and that of obedience the third.

By these vows man makes of himself a perfect sacrifice to God, he offers himself as a holocaust to His glory, surrendering into His hands, for ever, not only all earthly possessions that he has or might have, but even gives up his liberty and will, the most perfect immolation a human being can make.

Seeing how pleasing is this lifelong sacrifice to God, the Fathers of the Church, St. Jerome, St. Bernard, the Angelic Doctor and many others, have always called religious profession a "second baptism", by which the guilt and punishment due for past sins is entirely remitted.

"A religious lives more happily and dies more confidently," wrote St. Bernard, and well he may, for he knows that the three vows which bound him forever to the service of his Master have washed away all trace of a sinful past, that the evil deeds of his life, be they as numerous as the sands on the seashore, with all the dreadful consequences they brought with them, have been blotted out by the recording angel, and that his soul is as pure and spotless as when first the waters of baptism made him the heir of heaven: "Greater love than this no man hath," said the Saviour, "that a man lay down his life for his friends," and, adds the Apostle: "charity (the love of God) covereth a multitude of sins." By the daily crucifixion of his life, the religious makes this offering of all that is dear to him into the hands of his Friend and Master, a martyrdom far more painful than that of blood, but one which he knows will win for him a glorious crown.

One can easily understand, then, the determination of those who for one reason or another have been obliged to leave a religious house to enter again. Disappointment, delays, even refusal, seem but to increase their longing to give themselves to God, for they have learned in the convent the beauty and grandeur of a life which is "All Jesus", they have tasted their sweetness and realized the possibilities of immense holiness within its walls, and, like Isabella of France, who refused the hand of the Emperor Frederick to become a humble nun, they exclaim: "A spouse of Jesus Christ is far more than even an Empress."

XIII. The Harvest Of Souls

In the preceding pages we have seen briefly the nature and obligation of a vocation, and glanced at a few of its privileges and advantages. Yet some, even among Catholics, may be found to ask what need is there for so many priests and nuns?

Long ago, while yet the Saviour trod this earth, we read that once He sat by the well side, weary from His journeying. As He paused to rest, His gaze fell upon the waving cornfields stretching far out of sight, the ears bending under their load of countless, tiny seeds, each bearing its germ of life. To the eyes of His soul, devoured with a burning zeal, it was an image of the vast multitude of human beings He had come to save, of the souls of those with whom He lived and the myriads who would follow Him. Silently He looked at the solitary husbandman, sickle in hand, slowly gathering the sheaves of golden corn, then sadly turning to the disciples, He said, with a hidden meaning in His words: "The harvest indeed is great, but the laborers are few. Pray ye, therefore, the Lord of the harvest that He send laborers into His harvest."

The words died away, but their echo has never ceased to sound. "The harvest is great, but the laborers are few." Turn where we will, in no matter what part of the globe, and there we shall see still the harvest of souls, waiting to be garnered into the Master's granaries.

"Send me half a million priests," writes a Jesuit missionary from India, "and I promise to find them abundant work at once."

"For the love of God, come out to us. I have come across millions of men here in Africa who need but to hear Our Lord's words and deeds to become so many good and happy Christians."

Another, as he gazes at the teeming Chinese population around him, exclaims: "The ten thousand catechumens of my district would be a hundred thousand tomorrow if there were priests and nuns enough to instruct and receive them."

"The harvest indeed is great," a total Pagan population in the world of 995,000,000 (In 1910 edition, today more than 6½ billion.), or eight out of every thirteen of the human race, who have never heard the Name of God, each with an immortal soul looking for salvation. America, on the authority of Archbishop Ireland, with its forty thousand converts in one year; England, registering, at the last census, twenty million of her people as having "no religion", while from every town and village of our own land comes the cry for more Brothers, Priests and Nuns to labor in the fields "white with the harvest."

"Pray ye, therefore," still pleads the Saviour from the tabernacle, as He gazes on the vast work yet to be done, "pray ye the Lord that He send laborers, many and zealous, into His harvest."

XIV. An Appeal

Boys and girls, young men and ladies, with your young lives so full of promises opening out before you, have you no nobler ideals, no loftier ambition, than to spend your days in pleasure and amusement, while your brothers and your sisters look appealing to you for help? Lift up your eyes and see the harvest awaiting you, the most glorious work ever given man to do, the saving of immortal souls!

The day of Ireland's greatest glory was the time when the land was covered with a golden network of schools and monasteries; when her missioners and nuns were to be found in every clime and country; when every tenth Irishman and woman was consecrated to God and His service. "If our country would be born again," wrote Thomas Francis Meagher, "she must be baptized once more in the old Irish holy well." This is the work that lies before you, the work God looks to you to do, strengthening the faith that St. Patrick, St. Francis Xavier, St. Alphonsus and other saints left us, preaching the truth to an unbelieving world, sacrificing yourselves, as your ancestors did before, leaving home and friends, and, for the sake of God, giving your life that others may be saved.

A vocation is, indeed, the gift of God, but through love of the souls whom He longs to save, gladly would He bestow it on many more, if only they would listen to His voice or ask Him for this treasure.

Are you one, dear reader, at whose heart Jesus has long been knocking, perhaps in vain, inviting, pleading, urging? "The Master is here and calls for you"; He has need of you for His work. Follow Him bravely and trustfully, you will never regret it. But if you have not yet heard that voice, then remember His words: "Ask and you shall receive"; ask Him for a vocation, not once but daily, ask confidently, perseveringly, for He has pledged His word to hear you, so that you, also, may share the happiness of those who serve the Lord, and that "your joy" - like theirs - "may be full."

"One thing I have asked of the Lord, this will I seek after, that I may dwell in the house of the Lord all the days of my life." (Psalms 26:4)

A. M. D. G.
Ad Majorem Dei Gloriam
"For the greater honor and glory of God."

Appendix: Definitions

Active life: Pope St. Gregory the Great defines the active life thus, "To feed the hungry, to teach the ignorant, to correct the erring, to recall our neighbor to the path of humility when he becomes proud, to care for the sick, to dispense to all that which they need, and to provide for those entrusted to our care." The phrase active life is generally used in the antithesis to contemplative life which is in itself greater supernatural worth, but according to St. Thomas Aquinas, an active life may be become strictly obligatory (to earn a living, to escape temptation, succor the needy) and so more meritorious than the other. Active life or active works does not refer to mere bodily activity, which may be employed in agriculture or the arts, but to external actives carried on away from the monastery, by the cure of souls, preaching, giving retreats, conducting schools, etc. Thus, the English and other Benedictines who parishes pursue an active life the Cistercians, who farm the land attached to their monasteries, do not.

Active Orders: Those religious orders and congregations of men and women whose daily labors are the works of charity, whether spiritual, (preaching, hearing, confessions, giving retreats, the cure of souls generally) or temporal (the care of the sick, schooling children, bringing up orphans, etc.). Such are the Jesuits, the Redemptorists, the Passionists, the Christian Brothers, etc., among men, and the Sisters of Charity, the Little Sisters of the Poor, the Daughters of the Cross, the Ursulines, etc., among women.

Chastity: As a virtue it is that virtue which excludes all indulgence of and all voluntary pleasure arising from the sexual appetite in the case of single persons. Controls the use of such appetite according to the dictates of right reason in the case of married persons. It is thus seen to be either absolute or relative. It is thus seen to be either absolute or relative: "a man's intercourse with his lawful wife is chastity," said St. Paphnutius before the Council of Nicæa: on the other hand, a married pair are at liberty to agree to live in absolute chastity. Chastity must be distinguished from celibacy, and continence, purity, virtue. As a evangelical counsel, absolute chastity is voluntary undertaken by the clergy of the Latin Church when ordained subdeacon, and by monks, nuns, and other religious at profession in accordance with the terms of the profession. An act committed against chastity by one who has taken a vow of chastity, either by ordination, religious profession, or privately, is a twofold sin, against the virtue and against the vow.

Cloister/Enclosure: That part of a monastery or convent which has been canonically enclosed as the residing place of the religious. The restriction imposed by the law regarding this material enclosure. The extent of building enclosed is arbitrary and governed by requirements; thus the quire of the church is nearly always enclosed but the nave not, and there are usually public rooms at the entrance to the monastery itself: but the boundaries of the enclosure must be clearly indicated. Male religious may not leave their enclosure without permission of their superior but permission is freely given as occasion requires. Laymen may enter a monastery of men when invited to do so, but women are strictly excluded; both she who enters and the religious administering her ipso facto (automatically) incur excommunication absolutely reserved to the Holy See. Female religious with solemn vows are more strictly enclosed. No professed nun may leave the enclosure except with a papal indult, or being in danger of death, or on account of the other very grave evil. No one, male or female, clerical or lay, may enter their enclosure; offenders and those who admit them incur excommunication as above. There are the follow necessary exceptions: the bishop or superior of the order or their delegates when making a visitation: the confessor, to minister to the sick or dying; reigning sovereigns, their consorts; cardinals, and their attendant court; physicians and workmen when required. Under varying conditions a nun professed in solemn vows may receive visitors in the parlor where conversation takes place through a large grating, which may be curtained. The laws for nuns with simple vows are less rigorous unless the rule of their institute involves the strict enclosure; but even then they are not protected by the excommunications and other legislation of the papal enclosure of the solemnly vowed. Enclosed nuns engaged in active work freely meet outsiders within the limits of their school, hospital, etc.

Contemplation: An absorbing interest in some object, so that it is constantly thought about and engrosses the affections. In a religious sense it denotes the contemplative life, and the prayer proper to the contemplative life, although not all contemplative religious attain it, nor is it confined by any means to such religious. It is a prayer which dispenses with reasoning or discourse and with distinct perceptions of God, and concentrates on Him in a simple gaze and wordless act of love. It is to be noted that the elements of general contemplation, mentioned above, are here found, ie., the mind and will engrossed by God, so that the genuineness of contemplative prayer is supported by the analogy of certain facts of ordinary experience. Many authors distinguish two kinds of contemplation: acquired, which is the prayer of simplicity, and infused or passive, which is mystical union others; others refused to admit any such distinction, and hold that the mystical life is a normal development of the interior life, and that therefore all souls are called, remotely to it.

Contemplative life: One of the forms of the religious life, being a state, officially recognized by the Church, in which souls devote themselves to the objective worship of God and aim at attaining the prayer of contemplation. It is an austere life, to ensure that detachment from creatures without which union with God is not possible. Much time is consequently devoted to prayer, and external actives are excluded (contemplative order). Pope Pius XI sums up the traditional teaching of the Church concerning this life: "All those who, according to their rule, lead a secluded life remote from the din and follies of the world, and who not only assiduously contemplate the divine mysteries and eternal truths and pour out ardent and continual prayers to God that His kingdom may flourish...but who also atone for the sins of other men, still more than for their own, by mortification, prescribed or voluntary, of mind body – such must be said to have chosen the best part." But as all who follow this contemplative life are not contemplatives, so very many, whether clerical or lay, engaged in an active or semi active life are contemplatives, not only by being informed by the true spirit of divine contemplation, but also by attainment of that perfection of prayer. And in a yet more general sense, that man may be said to be contemplative who is concerned with ends rather than with means, with being rather than becoming, with things rather than appearances, who is contented, resigned, patient, and incurious, who recognizes but one cause in nature and in human affairs, and that is the First and Supreme, and whose apprehension of that cause tends to be passive, immediate, and independent of reasoning.

Contemplative Order: A religious order whose members are engaged in the objective worship of God to such a degree as to exclude the external works of the active life, and all else that could be a hindrance to divine contemplation. Such are the Cathusian, Camaldolese and Cistercian monks, and Carthusian, Carmelite, Poor Clare, Dominican (second order), and some other nuns. What exactly constitutes the contemplative life is a matter of some dispute, but even in the above strict sense certain monasteries of Benedictine monks, and most of Benedictine nuns, must be called contemplative.

Convent: (Latin for gathering) Used with the title abbot or prior means a monastic community in its corporate capacity, e.g., the Abbot and Convent of St. Gregory the Great at Downside. The buildings wherein lives a monastic community of monks, friars or nuns. The name is not given to the houses of the more recent congregations of men, Jesuits Passionists, etc.

Monastery: (Greek for the dwelling of a solitary) The fixed abode of a community of monks, canons regular or nuns, the name is extended to include houses of friars and of certain more recent congregations e.g. Passionists, Redemptorists, but never of Jesuits. Normally it consists principally of a church, chapter house, cloisters, refectory, cells or common dormitory, the superior's apartments, library and work rooms, guest quarters, parlor for visitors. For the canonical erection of a monastery with enclosure the permission of the bishop is always required in a certain countries of the Holy See as well; normally at least twelve religious must live in it. A monastery is generally an abbey or a priory.

Monk: (Greek for a solitary) One who by taking the vows of religion binds himself to the monastic life in its integrity. In the East all religious are monks, in the Latin Church only the members of the following orders: the Benedictine, Camaldolese, Vallombrosan, Sylvestrine, Olivetan, Cistercian and Carthusian. Canons regular are sometimes classified as monks, but the distinction between a monk and a friar is very sharp, both in law and in fact.

Novice: (novicius Latin for slave) One undergoing a period of probation, not less than one year, with the object of testing fitness for profession in a religious order or congregation of men or women. He is generally previously a postulant and becomes a novice by clothing with the habit of the order, which cannot take place till he has completed his 15th year. Certain conditions normally disable one from becoming a novice e.g., a subsisting marriage, parentage with dependent children or vice versa, lack of free consent, involvedness in secular affairs which cannot be avoided. A novice may freely leave or be dismissed without reason given at any time; at the end of his canonical period he must be professed, dismissed or may have a further trial up to six months. A novice may not renounce his property or any part of it, either in favor of his own monastery, order or anybody else, nor ordinarily does he defray the cost of his novitiate even if unsuccessful. A female novice must be specially examined by the bishop or his delegate as to her free consent, etc., before profession.

Noviciate: The period or condition of being a novice. It is followed by profession in temporary vows. The separate house or apartments in a monastery set apart for the use of novices. They must be entirely cut from those of professed religious, and choir and lay novices must occupy separate noviciates.

Nun: A member of a religious order or congregation of women. Canon law distinguishes between moniales (nuns strictly so called) belonging to institutes having solemn vows, and sorores (sisters) who have only simple vows. Nuns may also be divided according to the nature of their life into contemplative and active. Generally speaking, widows are received to monastic profession by way of dispensation. Penitents are eligible, but for the Carthusians complete bodily integrity is required.

Obedience: A moral virtue which enables one to recognize the authority of his legitimate superior and to carry out his orders accordingly; the superior may be God, a parent, a husband, a public authority, an employer, etc. The virtue inclines one to carry out the known will of the superior, without waiting to be told. But a command to do an act certainly known to be sinful may never be obeyed, however high or fundamental authority may be, and this no matter whether obedience be due by vow (e.g., from a religious), by contract (e.g., from a servant), by piety, (e.g., from a son or soldier) or in any other way. An evangelical counsel. The free renunciation, in whole or in part, to one's general independence of external action the better to follow Christ; a remedy against the dangers of self love, self esteem, and pride of life. The practice of the counsel may be given stability by a vow of obedience made to one's spiritual director or, more usually, to one's superiors in a religious order. The act by which a religious binds himself by the virtue of religion to submit to the direction of his superiors according to the rule and constitutions of the society. The vow of obedience is an essential element of the religious state. "The necessity which is consequent upon religious obedience is not a necessity of coercion but of free will, inasmuch as a man, although perhaps he would not be willing to do the thing commanded considered in itself, nevertheless wills to obey...and for this very reason that which he does is more acceptable to God." (St. Thomas Aquinas II-II Q.186 A.5 Reply 5)

Postulant: (postulare Latin to ask for) One preparing to be clothed as a novice in a religious house by means of a preliminary experience of the life. He wears lay clothes, or a cassock, and follows the usual community exercise under the novice master. The period of postulancy varies in different congregations, rarely exceeding six months, but for all women and lay brother postulants for orders with solemn vows it must be at least that period.

Poverty: This vow taken by a monk, nun, friar, etc., at profession involves the complete renunciation of all personal property. At simple profession the religious by this vow gives up his right to use any property he may have or acquire but retains the possession thereof (nor can his superior deprive him of it); he makes what arrangement he pleases for its administration and the disposal of income. At solemn profession he must dispose of its possession (not necessarily in favor of his monastery or order); his use of common property or disposal of what may come to him by inheritance, etc., is at the discretion and will of his superior according to the rules and customs of his order. The Fathers of Charity always retain the legal title to their personal property, but entirely give up the use of it; a solemnly professed Jesuit, Friar Minor, or Capuchin may not receive a legacy or inheritance and dispose thereof in favor of the order instead it passes to his next of kin.

Profession: A contract whereby a novice freely gives himself, by the taking of vows, to the religious life in a community approved by the Church. It may be solemn or simple, and this latter temporary or perpetual. Solemn profession is that which the Church recognizes as such and is always perpetual: any other profession is simple. Perpetual profession is not allowed except after simple temporary profession. The professed religious binds himself to tend to perfection by observing the evangelical counsels and obeying the rules and constitutions of his order. He must lead the life of a community and persevere in his state unless just cause, approved by his superiors, obliges him to return to the world. He shares in all the indulgences, privileges and favors granted to his community. Dispensation from religious vows, solemn or simple, is reserved to the Holy See, but superiors general can generally release from simple vows religious whom they dismiss, provided such religious are not in major orders. Solemn vows are rarely dispensed.

Religious: Any person, clerical or lay, male or female, who is a member of a religious institute. "A name common to many things is sometimes appropriated to that one to which it belongs to an eminent degree...Now, religion is the virtue by which a man does something for the service and worship of God. And so by a transference of epithet, they are said to be religious who have devoted themselves entirely to the service of God." (St. Thomas of Aquinas I-II Q.186 A. 1) Therefore, from the use of this word and such associated terms as religious life, religious house, it must by no means be inferred that the Church exalts the monastic and regulated life as the only really Christian life and monks and nuns as the only religious people; she merely says that, in the abstract, such the life is the highest of many forms of the truly Christian life.

Religious Life: "A stable mode of life in community, whereby the faithful undertake to observe, not only the general precepts, but also the evangelical counsels by means of the vows of obedience, chastity, and poverty." (Code of Canon Law #487) Religious are in a state of perfection and are bound to tend to perfection by practicing the counsels and submitting to the rules and constitutions of their order or congregation. They are to be content with the common life, even in the matter of food, clothing, and furniture. Superiors must see to it that their subjects make an annual retreat, devote some time to meditation each day, unless lawfully hindered, and carefully attend to the other exercises of religion prescribed by rule, assist at Mass daily, go frequently or daily to communion, and weekly, at least, to confession. They have all the obligations and privileges of clerics that are applicable to them. When not occupied in any outside work that may be entrusted to him, a religious lives in community with his brethren this is one of the chief external differences between the regular and secular clergy. Among the dissident orientals, especially where regular monasticism is moribund or dead, there are quasi religious who take vows of poverty and chastity and continue to live in their own homes, according to the practice of the primitive Church.

Secular Clergy: This ordinary clergy who pursue their work, principally parochial, living independently in the world, as opposed in the regular clergy who are bound by a rule and usually live in monasteries. The secular priest is the normal Christian cleric; he is bound by no vows except, in the Latin Church, by implication that of celibacy; he possess and enjoys his own property and is his own master except for canonical obedience he gives to his bishop; the episcopate properly appertains to the secular clergy, though for sufficient reasons regulars are often made bishops, especially in foreign missions. They take precedence of regulars of equal rank and are alone eligible for minor and titular prelatures, canonries, etc.

Seminary: (seminarium Latin for seed plot) A college exclusively devoted to the training of candidates for the priesthood. The usual course is six years, two of philosophy, four of theology, during which the student receives minor and major orders; his training includes dogmatic, moral and pastoral theology, holy Scripture, apologetics, ecclesiastical history, canon law, liturgy, and sacred chant. A candidate's duty is also to practice the ways of virtue for he will, after being ordained to the priesthood, have to guide his flock to a closer union with God according to ascetical and mystical theology. For as St. Augustine writes about lukewarm clerics who do not seek perfection: "God is more pleased with the barking of dogs, than with the prayer of such clerics."

Third Order: A branch of a religious order, whose members are laymen and women, pursuing the ordinary avocations of secular life. It is a true religious order, with noviciate, rule (which does not bind under pain of sin), office and habit (which must not be worn in public without permission of the bishop and the order; a scapular is worn under the clothing); its members are brethren and share in the spiritual life of the first order. It takes precedence of all confraternities etc., no one may belong to more than one at the same time, but may leave one at will and be admitted for a good reason to another. The general object of these third orders is to bring something of the religious spirit of the cloister into the world and to sanctify its members by striving after greater perfection in union with the fathers and nuns of the first and second orders; they are organized into chapters under a priest, but there are numerous isolated tertiaries; they are not bound by any vow; they may gain many special indulgences and other privileges.

Virgin Consecration: This solemn consecration was common in the early Church. The rite which must be performed by a bishop is contained in the Pontifcale Romanum. The nun is invested with a plain wooden cross, crown, black veil, and ring.

Vocation: (vocare Latin for to call) A call given by God to a soul. A fitness in the subject to bear the burdens of the religious life and a right intention of serving God in that life. Nothing more is necessary, no vivid inspiration or distinct divine locution: because the elements enumerated are definitely due to God's action, the fitness being produced by the natural causes under the guidance of the divine Providence, and the generous will to quit the world and devote self to God being clearly the work of grace. Priestly vocation, which is higher than religious, demands the same qualities in the subject, with the addiction of actual holiness of life. But here the qualities of the subject do not alone suffice. The priesthood belongs to the public order of the Church, and therefore external authority, in the person of the bishop, is the decisive factor in ecclesiastical vocation. It is the bishop's call that is the real manifestation of the divine vocation, for then, and not till then, is the candidate called by God as Aaron was. "It is better to go into religion with a view to testing oneself than not to go in at all, since this is the first step to stopping in it altogether. Nor may we say of a man who makes this experiment that he has 'looked back' (Luke 9:62) unless he has drawn back from something to which he was bound." (St. Thomas Aquinas)

Vow: A solemn promise made to God freely and deliberately to perform some good work or to embrace a higher state of life. The fulfillment of a vow is an obligation of the virtue of religion. Vows are public (e.g. the vows of monks and nuns) or private, solemn or simple. A vow binds no one but the vower, but the obligations of real vows, whereby property is dedicated to God, pass to heirs. Ordinaries can dispense or commute vows for a just cause, except those reserved to the pope. The only private vows reserved to the pope are those of perfect and perpetual chastity, and of entering a religious society of solemn vows. Vows pronounced under grave extrinsic fear unjustly inflicted are null and void. As impediment to marriage. The solemn vows taken by a religious, the vow of chastity taken implicitly on ordination to subdiaconate, and by special privilege, the simple vows taken at first profession by the Jesuit, are diriment impediments to marriage, and are practically never dispensed. The simple religious and private vows of virginity, of perfect chastity, of celibacy, to receive Holy Orders and to enter a religious order or congregation are prohibiting impediments only. Those bound by solemn or perpetual simple vows who attempt marriage, and their partners if they are privy to the fact, ipso facto (automatically) incur excommunication, simply reserved to the Holy See in the first case, to the ordinary in the second.

Made in the USA
Middletown, DE
01 March 2023

25944254R00027